21st CENTURY LIVES
WRITERS

Debbie Foy

WAYLAND

First published in 2010 by Wayland

Wayland
338 Euston Road
London NW1 3BH

Wayland Australia
Level 17/207 Kent Street
Sydney, NSW 2000

Editor: Julia Adams
Designer: Rebecca Painter
Picture researcher: Shelley Noronha

Picture Acknowledgments:

p2: Nick Cunard/Rex Features; p4: Daniel Deme/epa/Corbis; p5: MJ Kim/Getty Images; p6: Colin
McPherson/Corbis; p7: Rune Hellestad/Corbis; p8: Nick Cunard/Rex Features; p9: ITV/Rex Features;
p10: Colin McPherson/Corbis; p11: ITV/Rex Features; p12: Colin McPherson/Corbis; p13:
MGM/Everett/Rex Features; p14: Manou Riahnon/Rex Features; p15: Nigel R. Barklie/Rex Features;
p16: Rex Features; p17: Paramount/Everett/Rex Features; p18: KPA Zuma/Rex Features; p19 &
COVER: Lester Cohen/WireImage/Getty Images; p20: Rune Hellestad/Corbis; p21: Crispin
Rodwell/Rex Features

British Library Cataloguing in Publication Data:
Foy, Debbie.
   Writers. -- (21st century lives)
   1. Authors--Biography--Juvenile literature. 2. Children's
   literature--Authorship--Juvenile literature.
   I. Title II. Series
   809'.051-dc22

Printed in China

ISBN: 978 0 7502 6203 3

Wayland is a division of Hachette Children's Books, an Hachette UK company

www.hachette.co.uk

Contents

Philip Pullman
The Daemon Storyteller

On the red carpet! Philip arrives at the premiere of his Oscar-winning film, The Golden Compass.

> **"Lyra came to me as all my characters come to me, and I knew who she was at once. I knew what her name was and what she looked like, I could hear her voice. I didn't make her up. And I did make her up, but I didn't do it consciously. She just appeared. In the shed."**

**Interview with Philip Pullman,
guardian.co.uk,
10 November 2001**

Full name: Philip Pullman

Date and place of birth: 19 October 1946, Norwich, England

Education: Philip was educated in England, Zimbabwe and Australia, before his family settled in North Wales. He went to Exeter College, Oxford, to study for a degree in English.

Why he started to write: Philip has always been a compulsive storyteller. As a child he was forever crafting fantastical stories and telling them to his brother and friends. When he became old enough, he started to write them down.

Some popular books: *Count Karlstein, Ruby in the Smoke, Spring-Heeled Jack, Clockwork or All Wound Up, The Firework-Maker's Daughter, Northern Lights, The Subtle Knife, I was a Rat!, The Amber Spyglass, Lyra's Oxford, Once Upon a Time in the North, The Good Man Jesus and the Scoundrel Christ*

Awards and achievements: In 1996 Philip was awarded the Carnegie Medal for *Northern Lights*, and in 2001 *The Amber Spyglass* received the overall Whitbread Award. In 2006 *Northern Lights* had the great honour to receive the 'Carnegie of Carnegies' – chosen from all the Carnegie-winning books in the last 70 years. Philip's *His Dark Materials* trilogy was adapted and appeared at the National Theatre to great critical acclaim in 2003, and in 2007 the film of his trilogy *The Golden Compass* received an Oscar.

Writing style: It's proper torch-under-the-bedclothes stuff, full of action-packed adventure and a richness of imagination that will take your breath away!

Something you may not know about him: Every day, Philip Pullman writes around 1,000 words by hand on three sides of plain paper in his shed at the bottom of his garden.

Philip Pullman loves to tell stories. Here he is helping children find their own 'dæmon', while a cheeky black and white lemur perches on his shoulder.

When his stepfather died, Philip Pullman arranged for his ashes to be scattered through a stunning firework display. The ashes, distributed between handmade rockets, were crafted especially by a local firework-maker. After a final farewell the rockets shot into the night sky, scattering the ashes over the Firth of Forth in Scotland.

If this sounds as bizarre and fantastical as something you might encounter in a book, welcome to the world of Phillip Pullman – a writer whose imagination has enchanted children with his magical tales of fantasy, mystery and other worlds.

As a child, Philip's family moved around with his father's RAF job. But when his father's plane was shot down in Zimbabwe, his mother remarried and the new family moved to Australia. Philip and his younger brother spent hours inventing dramatic, intense and fantastical games, some of which they would continue for days, weeks or months.

After settling back in North Wales in his later childhood, Philip went to Oxford to study English. He was writing stories at the time, but turned to teaching in order to make a living. In the early seventies, he taught at a middle school in Oxford, and enjoyed putting on plays to entertain parents and children alike. Though he gave up teaching in the mid-eighties to pursue his writing, Phillip still has a passionate interest in education and holds firm opinions on how literature should be taught in schools.

He has written many fairytales (as he calls them), but his runaway success has been his award-winning *His Dark Materials* trilogy comprising *Northern Lights*, *The Subtle Knife* and *The Amber Spyglass*. The trilogy has resonated deeply with children and adults alike, and though it has invited deep discussion (and sometimes criticism) about the way that Pullman portrays God and religion, the trilogy remains one of the most well-loved, best-selling and influential works in children's fiction.

"If Pullman has a dæmon, it is a jackdaw, forever on the hop for something bright, a jewel, a screwed up Kit Kat wrapper, anything, to take home and store away. Nothing bores him."

Sally Vincent, on Philip Pullman's gathering of material, *The Guardian*, 10 November 2001

Michael Morpurgo
The Magical Storyteller

Michael's ideas for his books come from all around him: places, people and stories he hears. His eyes and ears are always open for inspiration.

❝I was an *Asterix* nutter! I loved the wordplay, the wacky slapstick of the humour. But I loved the stories as well. Words in large numbers still alarmed me, inhibited me, but stories excited me, set me free, made me laugh or cry, or both. I couldn't get enough of them.❞

Michael Morpurgo, on reading in his early teens, *The Sunday Times*, 2007.

Name: Michael Andrew Bridge Morpurgo

Date and place of birth: 5 October 1943, St Albans, Hertfordshire

Education: Michael attended schools in London, Sussex and Canterbury, Kent. After a period of army training at the military academy at Sandhurst, he went to the University of London to study English and French.

Why he started to write: Michael used to be a teacher and would read stories to his Year 6 class. Frustrated by how the stories failed to captivate the children, he began to make up his own.

Some popular titles: *Kensuke's Kingdom, Alone on a Wide, Wide Sea, Why the Whales Came, The Amazing Story of Adolphus Tips, The Butterfly Lion, War Horse, Private Peaceful, Running Wild*

Awards and achievements: Michael received the 1995 Whitbread Award for *The Wreck of Zanzibar* and the 1996 Nestlé Smarties Gold Award for *The Butterfly Lion*. In 2004, he was presented with the Red House Children's Award and in 2005, the Blue Peter Book of the Year Award, both for *Private Peaceful*. He was the Children's Laureate from 2003 to 2005, and in 2006 received an OBE for his services in helping young people.

Writing style: Michael often explores themes such as how it feels to be an outsider or surviving difficult circumstances. His settings are described vividly, and his characters can experience everything from the events of the First World War, the jungles of Indonesia, a desert island or the rugged Cornish coast.

Something you may not know about him: The Morpurgos founded the charity Farms for City Children in 1976. Over 60,000 children from deprived inner city backgrounds have had the opportunity to spend a week living and working on a rural farm.

Michael loves reading to children at public events. As a primary school teacher, this is how his passion for writing started.

At the age of 19, Michael married his wife, Clare, and began teaching in a local primary school. He enjoyed 'doodling stories' in his tiny study, but had no thoughts of becoming a writer. As a teacher he learnt that the best way to captivate a lively Year 6 class was to read to them. But one day, when he realised that the stories were no longer captivating them, he read the class some of his own. His passion for story-telling became obvious, and a career in writing followed.

Michael started to enjoy reading long after his teenage years were over, and looking back on his childhood, thinks that being force-fed 'proper' literature probably dampened his love of books. He challenges the idea of what children 'should' or 'shouldn't' read, and remembers the dismay of being handed books that were off-puttingly thick, or filled with endless lines of tiny text.

Many of his novels have already become modern-day classics, but it looks like Michael is set for even more success. *War Horse*, the epic story of a boy and his horse on the First World War battlefields was staged at the National Theatre in London and was a sell-out success. The film director Stephen Spielberg has bought the film rights and *War Horse* is now heading to Hollywood. So, as you reach for your popcorn while watching the Spielberg movie, remember to keep on reading, – and if you dream of becoming a children's writer – who knows? One day this could be you...

Living in the Devon countryside, listening to the music of Mozart and working with children have been the main inspirations that Michael Morpurgo needs to dream up and write his magical stories. His novels are the treasured favourites of children, parents, teachers and librarians all over the world.

Michael grew up in the leafy outskirts of London, with his brother, step-brother and step-sister, in a comfortable house that 'groaned with books'. Michael's mother inspired a love of poetry in her son, but when he got to school Michael grew to dislike reading and writing. As a young teen, he mainly read *Beano* and *Dandy*, *Asterix*, Herge's *Tintin* series, and the odd illustrated classic such as *Treasure Island* by Robert Louis Stevenson.

"This prize stuff is nonsense. You've written a fine book. And one day you'll write an even finer one."

The poet Ted Hughes who inspired Michael to keep writing when *War Horse* did not win the Whitbread Award, *The Sunday Times*, 2007

Malorie Blackman
Fantasy, Sci-Fi and Positivity

Malorie's ideas are motivated by some of her own childhood experiences.

> **❝I wanted to read books that had me in them. I loved fantasies, mysteries, love stories. It was the dearth of black children in those that made me determined to do something.❞**
>
> **Malorie on why she started writing, *The Times*, 2004**

Full name: Malorie Blackman

Date and place of birth: 8 February 1962, London

Education: Malorie excelled in English at her grammar school in Peckham, London. After a short and unhappy spell in Huddersfield studying business, she returned to London to study computer science at Thames Polytechnic.

Why she started to write: At the age of 28, Malorie decided that writing (instead of computers) was her passion. She took evening classes in creative writing and began to pitch her work to publishers. She was strongly inspired to write ordinary stories with a central black character – reminiscent of those she had read as a child.

Some popular books: The *Noughts & Crosses* series – *Noughts & Crosses*, *An Eye for an Eye*, *Knife Edge*, *Checkmate* and *Double Cross*. Other novels for children: *Hacker*, *Operation Gadgetman*, *Thief!*, *Pig-Heart Boy* and *Cloud Busting*.

Awards and achievements: In 2008, Malorie was awarded an OBE for her services to children's literature. She has won numerous prizes for her work including the 1998 Carnegie Medal and BAFTA (Best Drama) for *Pig-Heart Boy*, the 2002 Children's Book Award for *Noughts and Crosses* and the Nestlé Silver Smarties Book Award for *Cloud Busting*.

Writing style: Malorie's books often have elements of sci-fi or fantasy and contain strong, imaginative plots with gripping characters. Her writing is simple and direct, but the brilliant satire she uses to describe the world in *Noughts and Crosses* has been compared to George Orwell's *Nineteen Eighty-Four*.

Something you may not know about her: Malorie is a huge music fan and likes to listen to Outcast, Kanye West and Nickleback. She can play the saxophone and the piano.

One of Malorie's most well-known novels, *Pig-Heart Boy*, was made into a BBC television series.

created her hugely successful *Noughts and Crosses* series, describing the lives of a black 'Cross' girl called Sephy and a white 'Nought' boy, Callum.

Malorie grew up with her father, a carpenter and her mother, a seamstress. When she was 13 her parents split up and Malorie coped by inventing fantasies and writing secret poems about her feelings. She loved English at school and wanted to train as a teacher, but her careers adviser persuaded her that a business degree would be a better choice. In the end she got a computing qualification and worked as a database manager. She enjoyed her job and travelled all over the world, but craved something creative – and acted on it. She graduated from the National Film and Television School having studied acting, then turned to writing.

Malorie's writing output is as large as her enthusiam. She has written over 50 children's books, television scripts (including several episodes for the screen adaptation of *Pig-Heart Boy*), original dramas for CITV and BBC Education, and a stage play. Look out for her next works of genius – coming to a bookshop near you!

Malorie Blackman, the successful children's writer, needed a plaster one day and realising that the only ones available were pink, designed to blend with a white person's skin, made her think deeply.

Until then she had never set out to tackle race as an issue in her writing. Her award-winning novels such as *Pig-Heart Boy* and *Hacker* portrayed their heroes as ordinary, everyday kids who just happened to be black. But what would happen, she wondered, if society were inverted? What if black people were the ruling class, and white people were the poor minority who held the menial jobs? Based on this simple idea, Malorie

"She is hugely prolific... with an inexhaustible imagination providing strong, ingenious plots for any sub-teen. Reviewers who depress her with accusations of 'unbelievable' are missing the point: against an everyday background, her characters empower young readers to achieve what in reality they never could - solve the mystery, be smarter than the police, see the future and return."

Books for Keeps, www.penguin.co.uk

Jacqueline Wilson
Candy Colours and Gritty Realism

Jacqueline Wilson is one of the hardest working authors around. She regularly attends signings, gives talks and attends charity events.

"Sometimes I upset adult readers because I write from the child's point of view about parents who let them down. I can see that that might be unsettling."

Jacqueline Wilson, on the controversy her books has sometimes caused among adults, *The Observer*, 2 March, 2003

Full name: Jacqueline Wilson

Date and place of birth: 17 December 1945, Bath, Somerset, England

Education: Jacqueline went to primary school in Kingston-upon-Thames and Coombe Girl's School, Surrey. She excelled in English, but few other subjects and left school at 16 to work. At the age of 40, she took A-level English and passed with a grade A.

Why she started to write: As a child Jacqueline started to write as a cure for her boredom, and because she loved reading so much.

Most popular books: *The Story of Tracy Beaker, The Suitcase Kid, The Bed and Breakfast Star, Twin Trouble, Double Act, The Illustrated Mum, Dustbin Baby, Lola Rose, The Diamond Girls, Hetty Feather, The Lottie Project, Lizzie Zipmouth*

Awards and achievements: In 2002, Jacqueline received an OBE, and in 2005 became Children's Laureate. She has won or been shortlisted for numerous awards, including the 1995 Nestlé Gold Smarties Award and the 1996 Red House Children's Book Award for *Double Act*. She was awarded The Guardian Children's Fiction Prize for *The Illustrated Mum* and Nestlé Gold Smarties Award in 2000 for *Lizzie Zipmouth*.

Writing style: Jacqueline's stories are written in the first person. Her tone is confiding (often in a diary style), balancing serious issues and tough realism with fun and humour.

Something you may not know about her: Jacqueline holds the record for probably the longest book signing session in British history – with an amazing 8 hours!

When Jacqueline wrote her autobiography *Jacky Daydream*, people assumed it would be a book for adults. But she wrote it to answer many of the questions that children ask her about her childhood.

Ask any girl between the ages of 8 and 12 if they have read Jacqueline Wilson's novels or could at least pick out the distinctive candy-coloured covers of her books on a bookshelf, the answer would be, unanimously, yes. Her fiercely devoted fan base of 'tweens' consume her books with such a passion that she has sold over 20 million copies and has overtaken JK Rowling as the 'most borrowed author' in British libraries.

Jacqueline writes about subjects that most children's writers would shrink away from. Her main characters are modern children tackling poverty, disease, mental illness, depression and even death. But despite the dark side of her subjects, Jacqueline's delivery is chatty and sunny and her characters are presented as kids who are capable and resourceful enough to deal with the problems that life throws at them.

As a child, Jacqueline loved writing. At the age of 17, she found a job as a junior journalist with the Scottish publisher of comics *Beano* and *Dandy*. She moved to Scotland, where she wrote stories for a popular girl's magazine, *Jackie*. She married two years later and had a daughter, Emma. In the early years, the family had a hard time making ends meet, a situation she often deals with in her stories.

Though she had had some success with writing, it wasn't until the publication of *The Story of Tracey Beaker*, that Jacqueline was finally on the map as a writer. It led to three phenomenally successful BBC TV series, and her 1995 novel *Double Act* was also adapted for Channel 4 as a TV drama. Since then, Jacqueline has written roughly two novels a year, making her one of the busiest children's writers today.

With her love of black 'witchy' clothes and her trademark enormous rings that adorn each of her fingers, Jacqueline cuts quite a dash at personal appearances and book signings where her young fans turn up in their droves to meet her. Though she may not always be the number one choice for parents, kids' devotion to Jacqueline Wilson is total.

"It was a very nice opportunity because, being written in the first person singular, I felt that the illustrations should be done by the person telling the story, and that gave me the opportunity to draw in the spirit of a 10-year-old."

Nick Sharratt, illustrator of Jacqueline Wilson's novels, *The Guardian*, 2004

Anthony Horowitz
Creator of Schoolboy Fantasy

As a child, Anthony loved the Tintin books and began writing because he wanted to be like his boyhood hero!

"It's my *memento mori*. It tells me, don't play computer games, don't sit mucking about, just get on and write another chapter."

Anthony Horowitz, on the human skull given to him by his mother on his 13th birthday that now sits on his writing desk, *The Times*, 1 November, 2008

Full name: Anthony Horowitz

Date and place of birth: 5 April 1956, Stanmore, Middlesex

Education: At the age of eight, Anthony was sent to Orley Farm boarding school in North London. He later attended the prestigious Rugby School, then studied for a degree at York University.

Why he started to write: Anthony wanted to be a writer from the age of eight, realising that 'the only time when I'm really happy is when I'm writing'. Unhappy at boarding school, he made up endless imaginative stories to entertain himself and the other boys.

Some popular books: The *Alex Rider* series: *Stormbreaker, Point Blanc, Skeleton Key, Eagle Strike, Scorpia, Ark Angel, Snakehead* and *Crocodile Tears*. The *Power of Five* series: *Raven's Gate, Evil Star, Nightrise* and *Necropolis*. The *Diamond Brothers* series includes *The Falcon's Malteser, The Greek Who Stole Christmas* and *The Radius of the Lost Shark*.

Awards and achievements: In 2008, Anthony was nominated for the Booktrust Teenage Prize for *Snakehead*. He was awarded the British Book Awards Children's Book of the Year in 2006 for *Ark Angel* and in 2003 won the Red House Children's Book Award for *Skeleton Key*.

Writing style: Anthony's style is pacey and full of suspense as well as witty and intelligent. He is able to adapt his style to suit his subject matter – horror, fantasy, action or detective mystery. His work is well researched with realistic characters that children can relate to.

Something you may not know about him: Anthony's passion is scuba-diving. He has dived all over the world, including in the South China Sea, where he swam with hammerhead sharks!

Alex Pettyfer and Sarah Bolger star in *Alex Rider: Operation Stormbreaker*, an adaptation of Anthony's gritty, action-packed novel.

If you read about Anthony Horowitz's early years, you'd be forgiven for thinking you were reading a fictional account of childhood in the Dickens' era. Born into a wealthy, upper class family (his father was an assistant to then-Prime Minister, Harold Wilson), Anthony was raised by nannies and surrounded by servants and chauffeurs. And he hated it.

In a strange twist of circumstances, Anthony's father, threatened with bankruptcy, withdrew all his money from the bank, deposited it into another account under a false name, and then died almost immediately. Anthony's mother tried for years to locate the money – but it was never found.

Anthony was sent to boarding school at the age of eight. While being away from home was quite a relief, he was beaten regularly by the headmaster and so began inventing stories of great revenge to entertain himself and the other boys. He also often 'escaped' into the world of the glamorous James Bond films, which kick-started the idea later in his life for the phenomenally successful *Alex Rider* series, following the adventures of a super-spy teen who works for MI6.

Though Anthony's writing career first took off through television (he wrote the Bafta-award winning TV series *Foyle's War* as well as a raft of successful prime-time murder-mystery shows), his major success has arrived through his books for children. He feels that his unhappy childhood has provided him with a wealth of experience and inspiration for his writing career.

In 1988 he married TV producer Jill Green in Hong Kong. They have two sons – both of whom have been actively involved with research on his books. And Anthony takes research for his books very seriously. He has visited notorious crime gangs in Hong Kong for *The Power of Five: Necropolis,* operated a 150-metre crane opposite the Houses of Parliament for *Point Blanc* and travelled to Australia to research *Crocodile Tears.* So when you next pick up a Horowitz book you can be sure of two things. One – it's probably inspired from some personal experience or another, and two – it's a mind-blowing good read.

"Alex Rider's exploits have included snowboarding down an impassable Swiss mountain on an ironing-board cut into shape with a portable CD player that turns into a circular saw, outrunning six cars on a customised bicycle in Amsterdam ... Horowitz researches the technology and the stunts meticulously."

Amanda Craig interview, *The Times*, 2009

David Almond

Skellig's Maker

David Almond smiles for the cameras as he arrives to be presented with the Whitbread Award for his hugely successful children's novel, Skellig.

" **When *Skellig* came along, it seemed to come out of the blue, as if it had been waiting a long time to be told. At times it seemed to write itself.** "

David Almond on his famous work, *Skellig*, www.hodderchildrensbooks.co.uk

Full name: David John Almond

Date and place of birth: 16 May 1951, Newcastle, England

Education: David loved his primary school years, but hated grammar school! He studied for a degree in English and American Literature at the University of East Anglia.

Why he started to write: David had always known he wanted to be a writer. While he was a teacher, he began to have short stories published in magazines. But he needed more time to write, so he resigned from his teaching job and went to live in a commune in Norfolk.

Some popular books: *Skellig, Kit's Wilderness, Heaven Eyes, The Fire-Eaters, Clay, Jackdaw Summer, My Name is Mina*

Awards and achievements: He was awarded the Whitbread Children's Award for Novel of the Year and the Carnegie Medal for *Skellig. Kit's Wilderness* won the Nestlé Silver Smarties Award, *The Fire-Eaters* won the 2003 Whitbread Award, the Nestlé Gold Smarties Gold Award and was short-listed for the Carnegie Medal.

Writing style: The content of his novels can be dark and thought-provoking, but his style is engaging, powerful, rhythmic and 'musical'. Often set in the area he grew up, his writing sometimes contains north-eastern dialect.

Something you may not know about him: David's opinions on education got him in trouble with David Blunkett, the Education Secretary in 1999, when he called for 10 per cent of the school year to be free from the National Curriculum.

Skellig was successfully adapted for stage, and played to a rapt audience at London's Young Vic theatre.

The story of a dishevelled, irritable and arthritic man with crumpled angel's wings, living off spiders in a derelict garage came to David as he was walking along the road one day. He went straight home and began to write. The resulting novel, *Skellig*, was his first children's book after many years of writing for adults, and brought him overnight success.

It was a visit to a Newcastle school playground in which David saw seven-year-old children acting out the story of *Skellig* that David began to realise the potential for adapting his story for other audiences as well. Since then, *Skellig* has been made into a film, a stage play, an opera and a radio play.

David grew up in large family of four sisters and a brother. His father was an office manager and his mother a typist. He loved playing in the countryside around his home, but also had a passion for books and reading. He loved going to his local library and dreamed of one day seeing his books on its shelves. As a child David's favourite books were tales such as *King Arthur and his knights*, the stories of T. Lobsang Rampa and his sisters' Enid Blyton novels.

After university, David worked as a hotel porter and postman before deciding to train as a teacher. He hoped that the short days and long holidays would leave him enough time to write. He was wrong. After five years in a Gateshead primary school he quit teaching to live in a commune, housed in a ramshackle old mansion house in Norfolk. For a year and a half he lived on very little money and focused on his writing.

Since the late nineties, David has written a raft of successful titles that have become beloved favourites of children and adults across the land. Now living in the wild Northumberland countryside with his partner and young daughter, David can reflect that his dream of seeing his books on library shelves has gone way beyond his expectations...

"A work of exquisite heart-fluttering tenderness... an extraordinarily profound book, no matter what the age of the reader."

Chairman of the Whitbread Children's Award describing *Skellig*, 1998

Cressida Cowell
Dragon Mania

Cressida began to write the Hiccup books at home, using maps, lists, songs, report cards and drawings.

"It was a child-sized world which an imaginative child would find easy to imagine other different tribes living on... the kind of place where you might expect to see dragons sailing overhead."

Cressida Cowell on her childhood family holidays to the Inner Hebrides (the inspiration for Hiccup's adventures), *The Times*, 2005

Full name: Cressida Cowell

Date and place of birth: 15th April, 1966, London

Education: Cressida attended St Paul's School, London and Marlborough School in Somerset. She has degrees in English literature from Oxford University, and in graphic design from Central St Martin's, London. She also studied for her Master's degree in narrative illustration at the University of Brighton.

Why she started to write: She wrote her first story at the age of six. It was a love story about two hippos meeting on the Limpopo river. Writing the story gave her a great feeling of power. She could make anything happen! From then on she was addicted and wrote so many stories that her Year 3 teacher had to give her a new exercise book practically every week!

Some popular books: The *Hiccup* series: *How to Train Your Dragon*, *How to be a Pirate*, *How to Speak Dragonese*, *How to Cheat a Dragon's Curse*, *How to Twist a Dragon's Tale*, *A Hero's Guide to Deadly Dragons*, *How to Ride a Dragon's Storm* and *How to Break a Dragon's Heart*; The *Emily Brown* picture books.

Awards and achievements: *How to Train Your Dragon* was released in March 2010 as a major 3D animated film by Shrek creator, DreamWorks Animation. Cressida has also received the 2006 Nestlé Gold Smarties Award for her successful picture book *That Rabbit Belongs to Emily Brown*.

Writing style: Cressida's books are packed full of kooky, quirky, child-centred humour.

Something you may not know about her: Cressida is an old school friend of the popular children's writer, Lauren Child. Cressida's daughter Maisie acted the voice of 'Lola' in the first TV series of Charlie and Lola.

Picture this. It's late 2009 and Cressida Cowell is invited to the US by DreamWorks Animation – the studio that brought us *Shrek* – to promote the film of her best-selling book *How to Train Your Dragon*. She might be forgiven for pinching herself, because it is not often that a children's writer is offered such a dazzling opportunity. But then, it's not often you come across a book as richly imaginative as *How to Train Your Dragon*, or one that strikes the perfect balance (like *Shrek* does) between fairytale and modern-day comedy.

Cressida grew up in London, but spent her long summer holidays on a tiny, wild and deserted island in the Inner Hebrides in Scotland. She and her family (including younger brother and sister, Caspar and Emily) were dropped off by boat, and for several weeks they would have no contact with the outside world. The house where they stayed was lit by candle-light and there was no television or telephone. Cressida's father would entertain the children with captivating tales of Vikings who invaded the islands hundreds of years ago and of legendary dragons who lurked in the island's caves.

Cressida's first picture book commission arrived while she was studying for her Master's degree. *Little Bo Peep's Library* was published in 1998, and the highly successful *Emily Brown* picture books continue to captivate pre-schoolers today. But it was Cressida's vivid childhood memories of the island that inspired her to write and illustrate her first novels. The *Hiccup* series of books, featuring Hiccup Horrendous Haddock III, the reluctant Viking, and his equally reluctant dragon, Toothless, came to life in 2003. The first title sold 100,000 copies simply by word of mouth.

It is Cressida's child-centred humour, quirky typefaces and illustrations, ink blots and scribbles that attract your attention. Each book – though it may give the impression it was composed in a week – is a well-crafted work of comic genius and originality. And for Cressida, her journey has taken her from the Inner Hebrides to Hollywood. Now that's a proper fairytale ending.

"These are genuinely funny, cleverly written stories, and will be appreciated by boys and girls who delight in Cowell's clever use of language and dazzling similes."

The Hiccup series, *Publishing News*

Stephenie Meyer
The Vampire Queen

One of Stephanie's many 'red carpet' moments! Here, she is attending the Twilight premiere in Los Angeles.

> "I never planned to write a book. I wasn't planning on a career in writing, I wasn't thinking about stories I wanted to write down. But I had a dream..."
>
> **Stephanie Meyer,**
> **The Observer, 2009**

Full name: Stephenie Meyer

Date and place of birth: 24 December 1973, Hartford, Connecticut, USA

Education: Stephenie was educated at Chaparral high school, Arizona. She went on to study for an English degree at the Brigham Young University in Utah.

Why she started to write: One night Stephanie had a vivid dream. She felt compelled to write it down, and, with the encouragement of her sister, sent it to several publishers.

Most popular books: The *Twilight* saga: *Twilight, New Moon, Eclipse, Breaking Dawn*

Awards and achievements: *Twilight* was named Best Book of the Decade by Amazon.com and Publishers' Weekly Best Book of the Year. *New Moon* spent 25 weeks at number 1 on the *New York Times* bestseller list and *Breaking Dawn* sold 1.3 million copies in its first 24 hours of publication. The *Twilight* and *New Moon* movies have been worldwide box office hits.

Her writing style: Her language is simple, but her characters and settings are crafted so thoroughly that you can imagine yourself there. Her writing is also very compelling, capturing the sweetness of the love story as well as the feverish tension of the action!

Something you may not know about her: Stephanie's teenage years were not happy. Her skin has always been very pale, and she needed to undergo therapy after the other kids called her a 'ghost'.

For her army of devoted fans, Stephanie Meyer is a literary pop star!

She received numerous rejection letters from publishers, but one day, her manuscript fell into the right hands and what happened next was a phenomenon that would rock the literary world in the same way that JK Rowling's mega successful *Harry Potter* series had done earlier that decade.

Her first novel *Twilight*, published in 2004, gripped an audience of 'tweens' and teens who had grown out of the charms of the bespectacled wizard, and were looking for something a little more grown up. The story of Bella Swan, an ordinary girl who moves to Forks, Washington who meets and falls for Edward Cullen, a glittering young vampire, fitted the bill perfectly. *Twilight* fever struck as the novel and its sequels *New Moon*, *Eclipse* and *Breaking Dawn* (all cool black covers with splashes of deep crimson red) became some of the most talked about literary creations of the decade.

The *Twilight* saga has a legion of fanatical young fans, some of whom have been known to travel half-way around the world to attend Stephenie's book signings or personal appearances. What is remarkable is that though she is not a fan of horror stories, nor has ever read *Dracula*, she just happens to have hit on the best-selling vampire novels ever written and one of the biggest publishing phenomena of our time. The stay-at-home mum from Arizona is now one of the world's most powerful celebrities and a millionaire many times over. She has created stories that kids everywhere are just dying to sink their teeth into.

On 2 June 2003 when Stephanie Meyer woke up her life changed dramatically. The previous night she had had a dream about a girl and a vampire meeting in a rainy forest. The dream was so powerful she could not get it out of her head. Over the coming months she crafted the story in between changing nappies and making breakfasts for her three children, and then sat up late while the house was quiet to type it out onto the computer.

"Forget queuing outside bookshops wearing a pointy hat: Meyer's fans like attending stadium events known as Twilight proms, where they can dress up as Bella [and] swig blood-coloured punch."

Olivia Laing, *The Observer*, 2009

Eoin Colfer
Hitchhikers and Hi-Tech Fairytales

Eoin attends a book signing in central London.

Full name: Eoin (pronounced Owen) Colfer

Date and place of birth: 14 May 1965, Wexford, Ireland

Education: After studying at the Wexford Christian Brothers School, Eoin went to Dublin University where he studied for a Bachelor of Education.

Why he started to write: He developed an interest in writing at primary school where he was inspired by the Viking legends he heard about in history lessons.

Some popular books: The *Artemis Fowl* series: *Artemis Fowl, The Arctic Incident, The Eternity Code, The Opal Deception, The Lost Colony, The Time Paradox,* The *Atlantis Complex; The Supernaturalist, Airman, The Supernaturalist 2, The Hitchhiker's Guide to the Galaxy: And Another Thing...*

Awards and achievements: Eoin was awarded the Children's Book of the Year Award, the Whitbread Children's Award and the WH Smith People's Choice Award (all in 2001) for *Artemis Fowl.* In 2009 he was shortlisted for the prestigious Carnegie Medal for *Airman.*

Writing style: Dynamic and fast-moving. Eoin writes plots that have twists and turns, and are original and inventive, laced with plenty of humour.

Something you may not know about him: In his bestselling *Artemis Fowl* series Eoin has used his four brothers' names and character traits to describe four characters – who happen to be goblins!

  "When I started to write I had no intentions of making Artemis the central character; he was just the bad guy Holly was up against and that was that ... But then parts of myself started to go in, and he developed a conscience and it became a very interesting book to write."

Eoin Colfer on Artemis Fowl,
The Times, 10 January 2005

Eoin Colfer and his son, Finn, share a story together at home in Wexford, Ireland.

Eoin and his brothers grew up in Wexford, Ireland, with artistic, educated parents. After finishing his degree, he and his wife lived abroad for several years in Tunisia, Saudi Arabia and Italy. He returned to Ireland, found a job teaching in a primary school and began to write. His first novel *Benny and Omar*, published in 1998, was based on his experiences in Tunisia.

Though he'd had some success getting work published in Ireland, his family knew that his writing had the potential to be enjoyed by a much wider audience. When Eoin Colfer's four brothers (jokingly) threatened to beat him up if he didn't try to get his stories published, Eoin knew it was time to act. He sent off a manuscript that featured a 12-year-old criminal mastermind called Artemis Fowl. Within a matter of weeks Eoin Colfer's life had changed forever.

Fowl mania had arrived! Sales of Artemis Fowl books went stratospheric, and so, after ten years of teaching, Eoin resigned his job and with the support of his family, devoted himself to writing. With its genius anti-hero (Artemis), an edgy fairy (Holly), its fast-action plot and technical wizardry the series has the pace and energy of a PlayStation game. The *Artemis Fowl* series has famously been described as 'like Diehard but with fairies'.

News of Eoin's humorous and quirky writing style reached the ears of Douglas Adams' agent. Adams wrote *The Hitchhiker's Guide to the Galaxy* series but passed away leaving it unfinished. In September 2008 Eoin was commissioned to write the sequel and *And Another Thing...* – the sixth instalment of the highly popular series – was published in 2009, to great acclaim.

Eoin currently lives with this wife and sons in a house close to where he grew up in Ireland. He travels a lot, has great plans for his writing, is wealthy and successful but his feet are firmly on the ground. His brothers wouldn't have it any other way.

"It is Colfer's sense of humour that ... has earned him a place in children's hearts. Mulch Diggums, the dwarf who can unhinge his jaw to eat earth and expel it with devastating digestive force when his bum-flap is unbuttoned, is just one of the comic creations that make his novels must-reads."

Amanda Craig interview, *The Times*, January 2005

Other Famous Writers

Diana Wynne Jones

Diana was born on 16 August 1934 in London, the daughter of teachers. She was evacuated to Wales at the age of five when war broke out. In 1943 the family (including her sisters Isobel and Ursula) settled in Essex but endured an unhappy childhood. She eventually went to St Anne's College, Oxford, to study English.

Diana's books are often compared to the Harry Potter series, as they are packed full of fantasy and sorcery. Some of her most popular titles include the Chrestomanci series : *Charmed Life*, *The Lives of Christopher Chant*, *The Magicians of Caprona*, *Witch Week* and *Conrad's Fate*. Other popular titles include *Howl's Moving Castle* (which was made into a successful anime movie by the director of *Spirited Away* in 2009) and *Dark Lord of Derkholm*. The mother of three grown-up boys (the inspiration for many of her boy heroes), she now lives in Bristol, where she visits schools and teaches writing courses.

Lauren Child

One of the most talented author-illustrators of today, Lauren Child grew up in Marlborough, Wiltshire, the second of three sisters. Before she started writing she had a variety of jobs from waitressing to designing lampshades to working as an assistant for the artist Damien Hirst.

Lauren had a huge amount of success with her *Charlie and Lola* picture books that use photography (usually taken by Lauren herself), collage and quirky typefaces as part of the design. She won the prestigious Kate Greenaway Medal for *I Will Not Ever Never Eat a Tomato*, and *Charlie and Lola* was made into a BAFTA-winning TV series.

Utterly Me, Clarice Bean, Lauren's first novel for older children (9+), was a runaway success all over the world, followed by *Clarice Bean Spells Trouble* and *Clarice Bean, Don't Look Now*. Lauren has now sold over 3 million books, and has made bedtime reading utterly irresistable!

Darren Shan

Darren O'Shaughnessy writes under the pen name of Darren Shan. He was born in London in 1972, but moved to Ireland with his parents and younger brother when he was six, and has lived there ever since.

He began writing for fun as a teenager and bought his first typewriter at 14. From then on, he wrote plenty of short stories and a year later came runner-up in a script-writing competition. Darren worked for a cable television company for two years before deciding, at the age of 23, that he was going to be a full-time writer. His first children's book, *Cirque du Freak*, part of a vampire series called *The Saga of Darren Shan*, got rave reviews in 2000. He followed up with *The Demonata*, an equally terrifying series about demons. His books have sold nearly 15 million copies, establishing Darren as the 'master of children's horror'.

Hilary Mckay

From a very early age Hilary McKay was an avid reader. She often 'lost' herself in her books, and felt that the local library was almost as familiar to her as her own home.

Hillary was born in Lincolnshire and grew up with three sisters. After studying botany and zoology at St Andrew's university, she worked as a biochemist in a laboratory.

She loved her job but at the same time had a burning desire to write. After the birth of her two children, Hilary left her job to devote time to bringing up her children and to pursue her writing career.

Hilary's books are fun and lively. Her most popular titles are the *Casson Family* series and the *Charlie* series, but in 2009 she wrote *Wishing for Tomorrow* – a sequel to the timeless and much-loved classic *A Little Princess* by Frances Hodgson Burnett. It was a story that Hilary had always wanted to write since she was a little girl.

Saci Lloyd

Not many children's writers have the occasion to turn down Johnny Depp. However, Saci Lloyd did when his production company approached her in late 2009 about making her debut novel, *The Carbon Diaires 2015*, into a movie. Saci decided to go with the producers of the BBC series *Skins* instead. *The Carbon Diaries 2015* (and its sequel *The Carbon Diaries 2017*) already have a dedicated teenage following. The books feature heroine Laura Brown at a scary time when climate change has dramatically affected modern life.

Saci was brought up in Wales. After attending Manchester University she became a cartoonist, and toured America with a band before working as a television script editor. By day, Saci is head of media studies at an East London sixth form college. She has launched a new Facebook-style site through which students at local colleges can discuss climate change and politics.

Charlie Higson

London-based Charlie Higson may be a face you know from TV. He has appeared in *The Fast Show*, *Harry Enfield Television Programme* and *Bellamy's People*.

In the mid-nineties he began writing books for grown-ups, but when Ian Fleming's agent contacted him about writing a new James Bond series for younger readers, he saw his chance and took it. The *James Bond* series of books is set in the 1930s and is aimed at children from 9 to 12 years old. There are five novels in the series: *Silver Fin*, *Blood Fever*, *Double or Die*, *Hurricane Gold* and *By Royal Command*. In addition, Charlie is also working on a new young adult horror series – *The Enemy* and its sequel *The Dead* were published in 2009 and 2010.

While Charlie has had to accept that he will never play the role of James Bond in film, he has the thrilling mission of committing Young Bond to print...

Robert Muchamore

Robert's first 'proper' job was as a private investigator. He found it not nearly as interesting as it sounded, so he took some time off to visit his sister in Australia. There, he discovered his 12-year-old nephew complaining there weren't enough interesting books for kids his age to read. This spurred Robert to start writing and, by 2002, he had written his first novel, *Cherub 1.0*. After many rejections, it was finally published in March 2003 under the title *Cherub: The Recruit*. The novel won the Red House Children's Award in 2005 and was published in USA and Germany. In the same year, Robert resigned from his job as a private investigator and began to write full time.

Cherub has taken the 'tweens' book market by storm, and there are now 12 books in the series, plus four titles in a second successful series called *Henderson Boys*. Look out for them – they are gripping reads!

Index

21st Century Lives

Contents of books in the series:

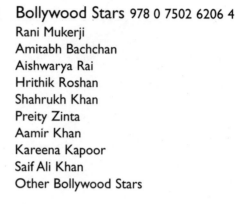